W9-AFF-415

I eat a rainbow

Me como un arco iris

Bobbie Kalman

 Crabtree Publishing Company
www.crabtreebooks.com

Created by Bobbie Kalman

Author and Editor-in-Chief
Bobbie Kalman

Educational consultants
Reagan Miller
Elaine Hurst
Joan King

Editors
Joan King
Reagan Miller
Kathy Middleton

Proofreader
Crystal Sikkens

Photo research
Bobbie Kalman

Design
Bobbie Kalman
Katherine Berti

Production coordinator
Katherine Berti

Prepress technician
Katherine Berti

Photographs
iStockphoto: cover (fruits and vegetables), p. 1, 13 (children)
Shutterstock: cover (children), p. 1, 3 (except apple, banana, and orange), 4, 5 (except apple, bananas, and orange), 6, 7, 8, 9, 10, 11, 12, 13 (except children), 14 (except lemon and tomato), 15 (except carrots, peas, and strawberries), 16 (bottom)
Other photos by Comstock and Photodisc

Library and Archives Canada Cataloguing in Publication

Kalman, Bobbie, 1947-
    I eat a rainbow = Me como un arco iris / Bobbie Kalman.

(My world = Mi mundo)
Issued also in an electronic format.
Text in English and Spanish.
ISBN 978-0-7787-8270-4 (bound).--ISBN 978-0-7787-8263-6 (pbk.)

    1. Food--Juvenile literature. 2. Nutrition--Juvenile literature.
3. Colors--Juvenile literature. I. Title. II. Title: Me como un arco
iris. III. Series: My world (St. Catharines, Ont.) IV. Series:
Mi mundo (St. Catharines, Ont.)

TX355.K343 2011   j613.2   C2010-904282-4

Library of Congress Cataloging-in-Publication Data

Kalman, Bobbie.
    [I eat a rainbow. Spanish & English]
    I eat a rainbow = Me como un arco iris / Bobbie Kalman.
        p. cm. -- (My world / mi mundo)
    ISBN 978-0-7787-8263-6 (pbk. : alk. paper) -- ISBN 978-0-7787-8270-4 (reinforced
library binding : alk. paper) -- ISBN 978-1-4271-9589-0 (electronic pdf))
    1. Nutrition--Juvenile literature. 2. Colors--Juvenile literature. 3. Rainbow--Juvenile
literature. I. Title. II. Title: Me como un arco iris. III. Series.

RA784.K2518 2011
613.2--dc22
                                                2010024912

Crabtree Publishing Company

www.crabtreebooks.com   1-800-387-7650

Printed in Hong Kong/042011/BK20110304

Published in Canada
Crabtree Publishing
616 Welland Ave.
St. Catharines, Ontario
L2M 5V6

Published in the United States
Crabtree Publishing
PMB 59051
350 Fifth Avenue, 59th Floor
New York, New York 10118

Published in the United Kingdom
Crabtree Publishing
Maritime House
Basin Road North, Hove
BN41 1WR

Published in Australia
Crabtree Publishing
386 Mt. Alexander Rd.
Ascot Vale (Melbourne)
VIC 3032

Words to know
Palabras que debo saber

apple
manzana

banana
plátano

blueberry
arándano

child
niña

orange
naranja

cherry
cereza

pepper
pimiento

rainbow
arco iris

3

red	rojo
orange	anaranjado
yellow	amarillo
green	verde
blue	azul
purple	morado

A rainbow has these colors.

Un arco iris tiene estos colores.

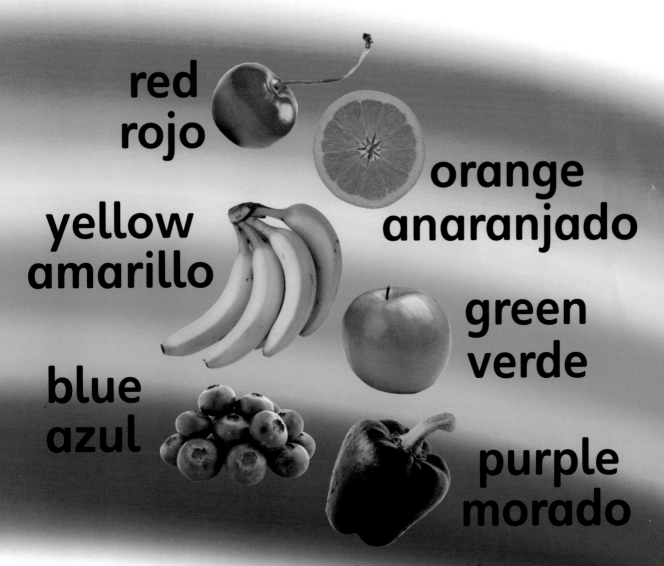

red
rojo

orange
anaranjado

yellow
amarillo

green
verde

blue
azul

purple
morado

Food has rainbow colors.

Los alimentos son de los colores
del arco iris.

5

cherry
cereza

The cherry is red.

La cereza es roja.

orange
naranja

The orange is orange.

La naranja es anaranjada.

banana
plátano

The banana is yellow.

El plátano es amarillo.

8

apple
manzana

The apple is green.

La manzana es verde.

blueberry
arándano

The blueberry is blue.

El arándano es azul.

pepper
pimiento

The pepper is purple.

El pimiento es morado.

I eat a rainbow every day.

Me como un arco iris todos los días.

orange
anaranjado

red
rojo

yellow
amarillo

purple
morado

green
verde

blue
azul

I am a rainbow child.

Soy un niño del arco iris.

Activity
Which foods are red?
Which foods are orange?
Which foods are yellow?
Which foods are green?
Which foods are blue?
Which foods are purple?

grapes
uvas

Actividad
¿Qué alimentos son rojos?
¿Qué alimentos son
anaranjados?
¿Qué alimentos son amarillos?
¿Qué alimentos son verdes?
¿Qué alimentos son azules?
¿Qué alimentos son morados?

corn
maíz

peas
chícharos

lemon
limón

plums
ciruelas

strawberry
fresa

carrots
zanahorias

tomato
tomate

pumpkin
calabaza

peppers
pimientos

15

Notes for adults

Eating naturally

I eat a rainbow introduces children to the healthful habit of eating natural foods of every color, every day. Nutritionists have discovered that we need foods of different colors to boost our immune systems, moderate our moods, and help our brains function better. Fruits such as apples, bananas, blueberries, red grapes, cherries, and oranges, and vegetables such as peppers, dark leafy greens, broccoli, tomatoes— and many more rainbow foods provide the body with important nutrients and fiber. This book can lead to a child's awareness that natural foods are what his or her body needs to function well and feel good.

Energy and colors from the sun

A rainbow is the sun's light broken into colors. You could show children how light breaks into rainbow colors by shining light through a prism. Our energy also comes from the sun. This energy moves from the sun through the food chain and into our bodies when we eat. Introducing the concept of energy from the sun will help children understand that eating a "rainbow" of colorful foods gives them all the energy and nutrients they need to keep healthy. That's why they are "rainbow kids!"

Notas para los adultos

Comer de manera natural

Me como un arco iris invita a los niños a formarse el hábito sano de comer alimentos naturales de cada color, todos los días. Los nutricionistas han descubierto que necesitamos alimentos de distintos colores para reforzar nuestro sistema inmunológico, controlar nuestro estado de ánimo y ayudar a nuestro cerebro a que funcione mejor. Frutas tales como las manzanas, los plátanos, los arándanos, las uvas rojas, las cerezas y las naranjas, y verduras tales como los pimientos, las verduras de hojas verde oscuro, el brócoli, los tomates y muchas otros alimentos que son de los colores del arco iris le proporcionan al cuerpo nutrientes importantes y fibra. Este libro puede servir para que los niños tomen conciencia de que su cuerpo necesita alimentos naturales para que funcione bien y se sienta bien.

La energía y los colores que provienen del sol

Un arco iris es la descomposición de la luz del sol en colores. Puede mostrarles a los niños cómo se descompone la luz en los colores del arco iris proyectando luz a través de un prisma. Nuestra energía también proviene del sol. Esta energía se traslada desde el sol a través de la cadena alimenticia hasta llegar a nuestro cuerpo cuando comemos. Presentar el concepto de la energía que proviene del sol ayudará a los niños a comprender que comer un "arco iris" de alimentos coloridos les proporciona toda la energía y los nutrientes que necesitan para mantenerse sanos. Por eso son, ¡"niños del arco iris"!